Lobos

A WOLF FAMILY
RETURNS
TO THE WILD

Brenda Peterson
Photography by Annie Marie Musselman

little bigfoot
an imprint of sasquatch books
seattle, wa

Newborn wolf pup brothers
hide deep in a den at Wolf Haven International,
a sanctuary in western Washington State.
They are born blind
and deaf—helpless.

Mexican gray wolves, also called *lobos*,
are rare and deeply endangered.
There are very few left in the wild,
so each pup is precious.

Once, they were hunted in Arizona, New Mexico,
and Mexico until nearly extinct.
But now scientists are helping lobos born in
US wolf sanctuaries return to the Southwest and Mexico.

The newborn pups are Mother
and Father Wolf's first litter.
The little lobos cuddle,
whimpering and warm,
squiggling and safe.
Tiny furry bodies, rough-and-tumble,
snuggle and wait,
always hungry to nurse on Mother's rich milk.

Father Wolf fiercely guards his mate and their pups.
He brings Mother Wolf food—deer meat
donated to the wolf sanctuary.

After twelve to fourteen days, the lobo brothers open their eyes.
Suddenly, their den feels too dark and crowded.
The wolf pups nip and wrestle,
restless,
eager to crawl outside.

Wiggling out of the den at last,
they blink in shock at their first glimpse of sunshine.
Now the pups explore their big world:
spring rain, mud, meadows, and sharp-smelling pine.

Clumsy, they trip and stumble over their own long legs.
The lobo pups must get much stronger to be chosen to
return to their native homelands.

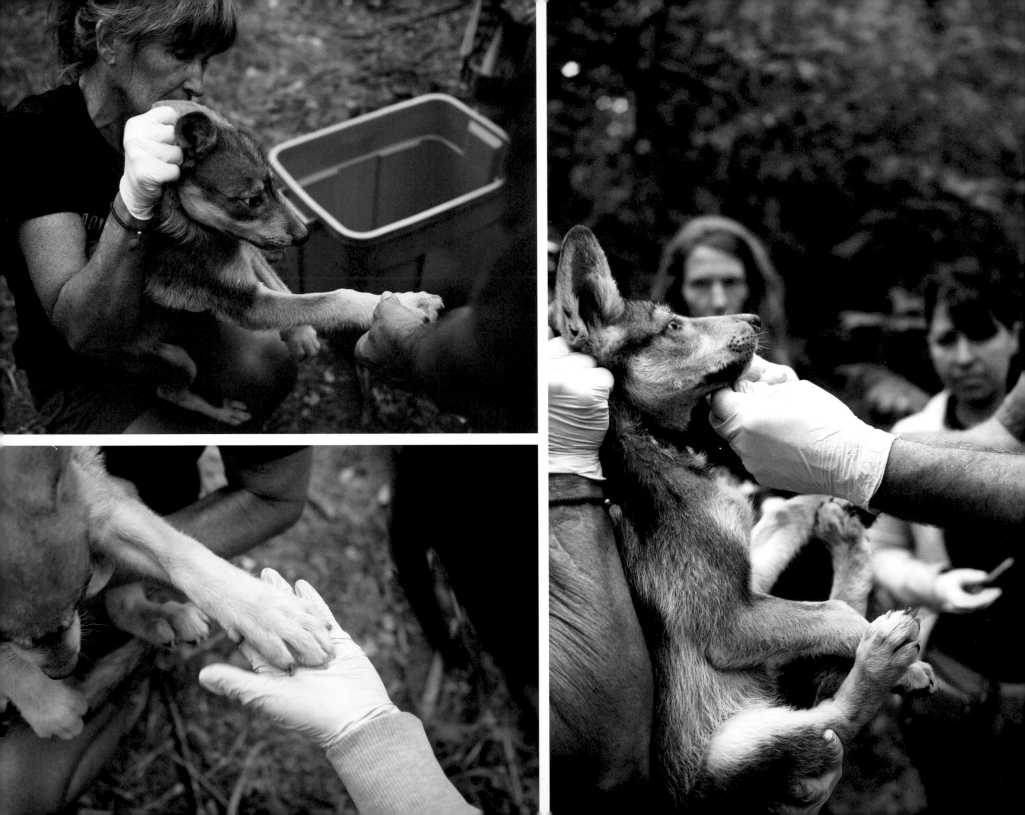

When they are six weeks old,
the lobo pups meet humans
for the first time. To wolves, we
smell just like skunks!

Very gently, a veterinarian listens
to each pup's rapid heartbeat:
lub-dub-lub-dub, lub-dub!

The little lobos tremble with fear.
Like all wolves, lobos are super scared
of people. In the wild,
we are the dangerous ones.

The vet and staff measure the wolf pups
for size and weight. "These pups are growing strong,"
the vet says, very pleased.

But soon two pups in another lobo family
suddenly die of parvo—a really contagious disease
that also harms dogs.
Everyone at the sanctuary is sad and very worried.

Happily, these brothers stay healthy.
The pups romp and run with Father Wolf,
who teaches his pups how to howl together.
Haunting harmonies.
Wolf music!

Playing with their parents,
the little lobos smell the sweet prairie grasses
and wildflowers of the Pacific Northwest,
and they chase a cottontail rabbit!

They hear a bird's flapping wings,
a scampering squirrel, a snake gliding
through dry grasses—even the rustle of a
willow's leaves six miles away.

All summer, the lobo pups grow tall and robust.
A favorite game they play with their father is to
jump on his back and jaw wrestle, play-fighting
with their open mouths.

By fall, the five-month-old lobos are no longer little.
Now they are almost as big
as their mother and father. For winter,
their fur grows thick and warm.
It easily sheds snow and rain.

The next spring, when the pups are a year old,
everything changes for the wolf family.

"The US Fish and Wildlife Service has chosen *our*
wolf family to return to the wild!" Wolf Haven's director
announces to the staff.
"But their trip will be scary—and dangerous."

Outside, all the wolves howl.
What's up? they seem to be saying.
Silently, a few of the trained sanctuary staff members
tiptoe into the lobo enclosure.

The gentle touch of a padded pole on Father Wolf's shoulder
signals him to crouch down.
He knows this touch.
This is how the medical staff catches wolves for exams.
A blue face mask is slipped
over Father Wolf's face to calm him,
like blinders on a horse.

Like a quick and quiet dance,
the staff catches each of the lobos in the family.
Carefully, each wolf is lifted
into its own kennel. They are ready
for their heroic journey.
First stop: Arizona!

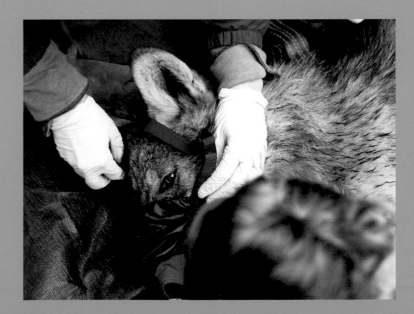

Inside her travel kennel,
Mother Wolf is trembling and terrified!
Her nose drips; her ears perk.
But she hears her pups snuffling
and smells them, safe around her.
That comforts her.

In a big van on the freeway to the airport,
the lobos hear shocking noises.
Car horns honk. Huge trucks screech and rumble.
They sniff the air, picking up strange new smells.
Greasy asphalt, exhaust fumes, junk food scraps—
what horrible smells for such sensitive wolf noses!

At the airport cargo dock, the lobo family is loaded
as baggage. No tranquilizers. It's too risky.
The wolves must stay wide-awake so they don't
get airsick and choke.
It's very cold and dark in the baggage compartment.
Passengers on that plane to Phoenix
have no idea there are wolves
traveling through the sky with them!

For twenty-eight hours, they travel—by plane and then by van,
all night through the desert.
The wolf family cowers in their kennel dens.
They are stiff and scared.

When at last they reach their destination,
the Ladder Ranch in southern New Mexico,
the lobos are too frightened
to leave their kennels.

But Mother Wolf is courageous.
She bursts out of her kennel into a spacious
field. Here is a strange new landscape—
wide blue mesas and mountains—
where they will get ready for their release into the wild.

Father Wolf and the lobo brothers
soon follow her lead.
The lobo family smells the sagebrush and the crisp, dry air.
The wolves leap and
splash together in a cold creek.

A big surprise at the Ladder Ranch!
Mother Wolf is pregnant again.
By early summer, newborn lobo
pups join the family.
The older lobos babysit
their new brothers and sisters,
playing and racing around with them.

It's all about family as the
wolves explore high plateaus and forests.
Mother and Father Wolf teach their lobo pups
how to hunt rabbits. One of the older pups leaps
and catches a raven flying too low.

All summer and fall, the wolf family
is watched over, in their large habitats,
by researchers hidden behind blinds.
Remote cameras catch the blur
of a pup racing by or Father Wolf stalking a gopher.
The lobos are still fed wild game by staff,
but they are beginning to hunt on their own.

Then one winter day,
everything changes all over again.
Mexican scientists ask to bring this wolf family
into their remote high-mountain wilderness,
far away from people.

There are only thirty lobos left
surviving in all of Mexico,
so they desperately need the new wolf family.
This would be the largest wild release of lobos
in US and Mexican history!

The lobo family is once more carefully caught up.
In pickups, they endure another long journey.

Traveling in his kennel,
one of the yearlings
gazes out, sniffing. He tastes the cold air
rushing by him. Does he sense that his
family will soon be free?

All eleven kennels are lined up together
in the Mexican wilderness.
The release team of scientists softly counts out,
"Uno, dos, tres!"
They open the kennel doors for the pups first.

Not one wolf jumps out!

The lobos are weary and cramped from
their long journey. They sniff the forest.

Mother Wolf races out of her kennel.
Sure enough, Father Wolf follows his mate.
But most of the little lobos are
still too frightened to run free.

"Let's keep the crate gates open and leave them overnight," a scientist
says. "Maybe they're too afraid with us here."
It's good that the lobos are still so frightened of people.
That caution—and their close family—
will keep them safe in the wild.

The next day, the scientists return and discover
that every kennel is empty!
Cameras in the trees are all that capture the lobos now,
as they roam their new mountain home together,
running through the soil.

They are welcome here
where they were first called *los lobos*.

Mother and Father Wolf
and their nine lobo pups are finally
and happily free
and what they were born to be:
wild!

The Story of Mexican Gray Wolves

Mexican gray wolves, also known as *lobos*, are endangered. The very few lobos left in the wild desperately need to mate with new wolf families. Wolf Haven International, in Washington State, and other US wolf sanctuaries, like New York's Wolf Conservation Center and Missouri's Endangered Wolf Center, are participating in the Mexican Wolf Species Survival Plan (MWSSP). This federal program reintroduces lobos to their native ranges in Mexico and the southwestern United States. Dozens of Mexican gray wolves have already been released back into the wild.

This book is based on the true story of Hopa (also known as F1222) and Brother (M1067), and their three male pups. Born at Wolf Haven in the spring of 2015, the pups are part of the MWSSP. When the pups were a year old, in 2016, the family made the perilous twenty-eight-hour pilgrimage by plane and van from the sanctuary to Ted Turner's spacious Ladder Ranch (a prerelease site) in New Mexico.

When Hopa endured this long journey, no one, not even the vet, knew that she was pregnant. At the Ladder Ranch, she gave birth to a second litter of six healthy pups. While the eleven wolves were waiting to return to the wild, Hopa and Brother taught the pups how to hunt for themselves, chasing down ravens and rabbits for a tasty meal. Meanwhile, the Ladder Ranch staff waited hopefully for permits to release the wolves somewhere in their native land.

In December 2016, the eleven-member lobo family took another long journey, this time to a remote forest in Mexico. For the first few weeks after their release, scientists left out roadkill for the wolves to eat. But very soon, the lobos hunted for themselves in that wilderness, full of white-tailed deer and other game. Now, the wolf family is finding other Mexican wolves nearby and flourishing in their native homeland.

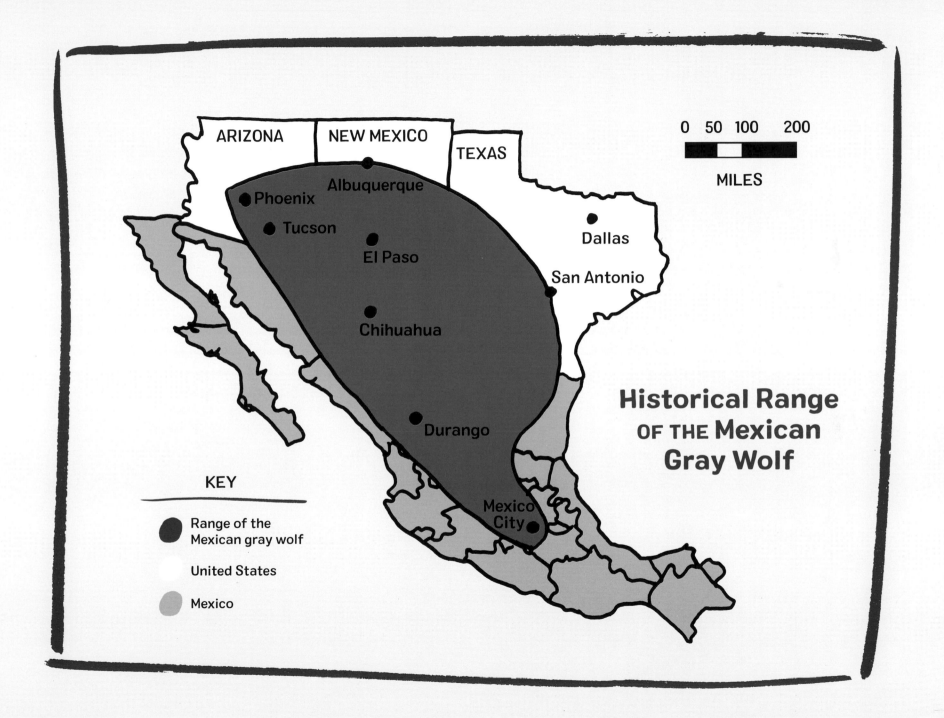

Historical Range OF THE Mexican Gray Wolf

ARIZONA

NEW MEXICO

TEXAS

0 50 100 200
MILES

Phoenix
Albuquerque
Tucson
El Paso
Dallas
San Antonio
Chihuahua
Durango
Mexico City

KEY

● Range of the Mexican gray wolf

United States

Mexico

Wolf Facts

 Lobos are the smallest of all gray wolves.

 As pups grow, their eyes change from blue to gold.

 At Wolf Haven, lobos were fed deer and elk meat, pumpkins, and *bloodsicles* by sanctuary staff.

 Wolves first came to North America by crossing the Bering Land Bridge.

 Wolves have a wide field of view, which helps with scanning their surroundings.

 Wolves move easily in a "harmonic gait"—their back paws fall exactly where their front paws have already landed. This conserves energy.

 Scent is a wolf's super-power. Their sense of smell is one hundred times better than humans'.

 Lobos' keen eyes see better than any dog.

 In the wild, wolves can travel twenty to thirty-five miles a day.

Timeline

Hopa (Mother Wolf) and Brother (Father Wolf) become the parents of three male pups.

The pups first meet a vet and staff for exams at eight, twelve, and sixteen weeks.

March 2015	April 2015	May–July 2015	April 2016

The pups explore their den and poke their heads out at three weeks old.

Three pups and their parents are transported to the Ladder Ranch in New Mexico.

When a dog licks your face, that's an instinct from the dog's hungry wolf ancestors.

Little lobos' sense of smell tells whether a visitor was recent or long ago, male or female, friendly or not.

Hopa is pregnant again and gives birth to a second litter of six lobos!

Now eleven-strong, the wolf family plays together, getting ready for their return to the wild. Yearling wolves help the new pups.

June 2016   **June–August 2016**   **September–November 2016**   **December 2016**

The wolf family quickly adapts to their native Southwest homeland—hunting and roaming the very large prerelease Ladder Ranch. They have very little human contact.

The lobo family makes the long journey to Mexico's remote mountain forests—and the lobos are at last FREE!

BRENDA

For future generations of lobos. And for the children—Analise, Barrett, and James. May they all thrive!

ACKNOWLEDGMENTS: Gratitude for the devoted staff of Wolf Haven International and all those who work to make the Species Survival Plan a success in returning wolf families to the wild. Many thanks to Gary Luke, Christy Cox, and Bridget Sweet of Sasquatch; my wonderful literary agent, Sarah Jane Freymann; Marlene Blessing; and Tracey Conway—all wolf people.

ANNIE MARIE

This book is for Chicken, my faithful dog of fourteen years, who has traveled with me on countless adventures including my work on *Wolf Haven* and *Lobos*. And for Maggie, my mom, who taught me to love animals as if they were human, to speak to them, and to listen carefully in the forest so as not to miss anything magical. And for all the women and soon-to-be women, may you have faith and strength and love through it all. And so many kisses to Wendy, Diane, Brenda P., Jim, and all my friends at Wolf Haven International, who made it all happen in the first place.

Copyright © 2018 by Brenda Peterson

Photographs copyright © 2018 by Annie Marie Musselman, with the exception of the following credits: Justin Hebert (pages 4, 27), US Fish and Wildlife Service (pages 5, 6), Jordi Mendoza/CONANP (page 19), Wolf Haven International (page 22)

Illustrations: © Creative Market | ECHOFOXX – Hand Drawn Nature Vector Pack (pages 3, 4, 9, 13), © iStock.com | mirquurius – Sign of howling wolf (pages 10, 26)

Manufactured in China by C&C Offset Printing Co. Ltd. Shenzhen, Guangdong Province, in May 2018

Published by Little Bigfoot, an imprint of Sasquatch Books

22 21 20 19 18   9 8 7 6 5 4 3 2 1

Editor: Christy Cox
Production editor: Bridget Sweet
Design: Bryce de Flamand
Cover photograph: Annie Marie Musselman
Copyeditor: Elizabeth Johnson

Library of Congress Cataloging-in-Publication Data
Names: Peterson, Brenda, 1950- author. | Musselman, Annie Marie, photographer.
Title: Lobos : a wolf family returns to the wild / Brenda Peterson ; photography by Annie Marie Musselman.
Description: Seattle, WA : Little Bigfoot, an imprint of Sasquatch Books, [2018]
Identifiers: LCCN 2017041817 | ISBN 9781632170842 (hardcover)
Subjects: LCSH: Mexican wolf--Reintroduction--Juvenile literature. | Mexican wolf--Conservation--Juvenile literature. | Endangered species--Juvenile literature.
Classification: LCC QL737.C22 P465 2018 | DDC 599.77--dc23
LC record available at https://lccn.loc.gov/2017041817

ISBN: 978-1-63217-084-2

Sasquatch Books
1904 Third Avenue, Suite 710 | Seattle, WA 98101
(206) 467-4300 | www.SasquatchBooks.com

BRENDA PETERSON is a National Geographic author, novelist, and memoirist, whose eighteen books include *Living by Water*, *I Want to Be Left Behind*, and *Your Life Is a Book*. Her work has appeared in the *New York Times*; *Orion*; the *Huffington Post*; *O, The Oprah Magazine*; and on NPR. BrendaPetersonBooks.com

ANNIE MARIE MUSSELMAN finds inspiration in the connection between humans and animals. Her last book, *Wolf Haven: Sanctuary and the Future of Wolves in North America*, documents a sanctuary for wolves and was the inspiration for her work in *Lobos*. Her pictures have appeared in the *New Yorker*, *Audubon*, *Outside*, *National Geographic*, and *Smithsonian*, among others. AnnieMusselman.com